# The Legacy of César Chávez

by Gretchen McBride

Scott Foresman
is an imprint of

Glenview, Illinois • Boston, Massachusetts • Chandler, Arizona
Upper Saddle River, New Jersey

Every effort has been made to secure permission and provide appropriate credit for photographic material. The publisher deeply regrets any omission and pledges to correct errors called to its attention in subsequent editions.

Unless otherwise acknowledged, all photographs are the property of Scott Foresman, a division of Pearson Education.

Photo locators denoted as follows: Top (T), Center (C), Bottom (B), Left (L), Right (R), Background (Bkgd)

Opener: Getty Images; 1 Getty Images; 3 Corbis, AP/Wide World Photos; 4 Corbis; 7 Corbis; 8 ©Claver Carroll/OSF Limited; 9 Corbis; 10 Corbis; 13 Special Collections, Stanford University Libraries; 15 Getty Images; 17 Getty Images, Take Stock Images; 19 Take Stock Images; 20 Dos Mundos; 22 Take Stock Images

ISBN 13: 978-0-328-51640-7
ISBN 10:      0-328-51640-6

3 4 5 6 7 8 9 10 V0N4 13 12 11 10

César Estrada Chávez
(1927–1993)

# César Chávez

After a life filled with struggle and triumph, misery and happiness, César Chávez died unexpectedly at age sixty-six. César was in San Luis, Arizona, on union business, when he passed away due to natural causes.

Although there had been many long journeys in his life, César died not far from the farm his family had lost in the Great Depression of the 1930s. The family farm was a place that held happy memories of hard work rewarded, independence, and self-respect.

César met many hardworking people living under difficult circumstances during his lifetime. César wanted these people to experience some of the good things in life that he saw as possible.

César's grandfather, Cesario Chávez, was born in Chihuahua, Mexico. His life was one of servitude, or forced labor, on a *hacienda,* or ranch. He worked as a ranch hand to pay the owner of the hacienda so that his days of servitude would be over. But the owner took so much from the wages of his *peones,* or farm workers, for room and board that Cesario could never save any money.

## Deep Roots

Finally, in the late 1880s, Cesario ran away. Crossing the Rio Grande into Texas, he made his way to Arizona. Cesario worked hard and saved money for a small ranch. The land he bought was near Yuma, Arizona. It was desert land, but the new dam that was being built in the Gila River valley would provide irrigation for the crops. Cesario would finally be his own master.

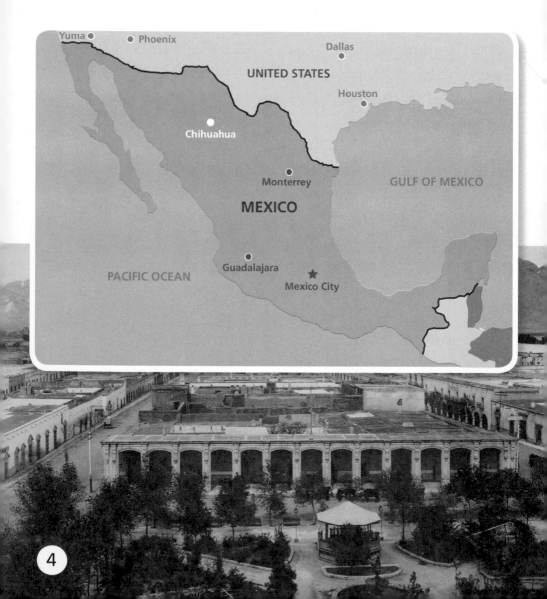

Cesario met his wife in the United States. Her family was also from Mexico. Dorotea—or "Mama Tella" as her grandchildren would call her—was literate. She had learned to read and write both Spanish and Latin in a Catholic orphanage in Mexico. Eventually, she would pass on her education to her children and then her grandchildren. Cesario and Dorotea would have fifteen children, including César's father, Librado.

Cesario and Dorotea built a large adobe farmhouse with thick walls to keep out the heat of the Arizona desert's summer days and the cold of winter nights. All of the children worked on the farm as they grew up.

When Librado was thirty-eight years old, he married Juana Estrada. Her family had come to the United States from the same area of Mexico as Librado's father. The couple owned and ran a small grocery store, a garage, and a pool hall. They also raised a family. Their second child, César Estrada Chávez, was born on March 31, 1927.

César's grandfather moved from Chihuahua, Mexico (pictured), to land near Yuma, Arizona.

# Growing Strong

There would be difficult—even terrible—times ahead for the Chávez family, but César's early years gave him many pleasures, and the memory of those years would later help to keep him strong.

His father taught César about farming. His mother, like his grandmother, was a religious person, and she passed on her values to her children. From her, César learned that instead of fighting, it was best to "turn the other cheek." She taught him that he did not need to resort to violence; instead, he should use his mind to find a solution to a problem. This lesson would be one of the most important of César's life.

He and his brothers helped with the farming and all three of the family businesses. César liked the freedom he had to roam the family farm. He and his brother Richard swam, hiked, and explored at will. They loved to build forts for fun out on the open land.

In October 1929, on Wall Street in New York City—very far from the Chávez's home—the stock market "crashed." Many people lost all of their money. Businesses failed and even banks closed all over the United States.

This economic disaster also reached the Chávez family. By 1932, they could no longer pay their bills. They lost their businesses. Then a great drought came. With no rain, the states of the Great Plains turned into a "dust bowl." Farms failed. The Chávez family could not pay the taxes on their land, and they lost their beloved farm. It was 1937. César Chávez was ten years old.

The soil that had produced good crops in the past turned into useless dust during the long drought of the 1930s.

# The Migrant Life

The Chávez family packed up their belongings and headed to California to find work. César's father hoped they could earn enough money to recover their farm.

Migrant workers, such as the Chávez family, moved from place to place, following the seasonal crops. They lived in rented houses that were often shacks. Usually, their basic living expenses ate up the low wages they earned picking grapes, lettuce, peas, or beans. The labor was **grueling,** workers often spent the entire day crouched, or bent low, to the ground.

Even the children worked in the fields, attending school only once in a while. César was fifteen years old when, after attending more than thirty different schools, he completed the eighth grade. He decided then that he must concentrate on earning money for the family and did not go back to school.

**Like these workers, César and his family worked long hours in fields that were not their own.**

César and his family often had
to live in shacks such as these.

In addition to the hardships of the road and field,
the Chávez family also suffered from **discrimination**
because of their Mexican heritage. In some small
towns in California, businesses hung out signs saying
"Whites Only." Once, César watched as his father was
cursed at and thrown out of a café where he had gone
for a cup of coffee. César would never forget the pain
he saw in his father's eyes.

Along with discrimination, the Chávez family and
other workers faced very poor working conditions.
Sometimes there were **strikes** in the fields. The
workers would stop working to protest their terrible
working conditions, low wages, and other unfair
treatment. César and his family often participated.
*"Huelga!"* the people would shout. Strike!

## Changing Times

In 1944 the United States was in the middle of World War II. César Chávez was seventeen. He and his family were still living the life of migrant workers, and their dream of buying back the family farm had long ago faded away. César decided that he had to make a change in his life. There were few opportunities for a young Mexican American man with little education, so César decided to join the U.S. Navy.

If, in joining the navy, César expected to escape the discrimination he suffered in California, he was disappointed. But César was learning from all his experiences—bad and good—and he would use what he learned to better the lives of many people.

When César returned to California after the end of World War II, he did not want to go back to work in the fields. The Great Depression was over, but no one wanted to give a good job to a young Mexican American man with only an eighth-grade education. César had to return to harvesting grapes.

But returning to California did bring César back to Helen Fabela. She was a young woman whom he had met a few years earlier when he was a teenager. In 1948 Helen and César married. The couple lived in a one-room shack with no electricity or running water.

But change was on the horizon. At first, the whole Chávez family tried renting a farm in San Jose to grow strawberries. This did not prove profitable, but it was better than life on the road. Finally, after César and Richard had worked at a rainy northern California lumber mill for a while, the Chávez family returned to sunny San Jose, where César got work at another lumber mill.

**César Chávez discovered that Mexican Americans also suffered from discrimination in the navy.**

## Sal Si Puedes
## "Get out if you can"

Within San Jose there was a *barrio,* or community of Spanish-speaking people, called *Sal Si Puedes.* This means, loosely translated, "Get out if you can." Most residents of the barrio hoped that one day they would escape from the crowded narrow strip of land. César, Helen, and their three children moved to *Sal Si Puedes* in 1952. In this unlikely place, César would meet two men who would influence his life greatly.

Father Donald McDonnell, the Catholic priest in the barrio, sympathized with the troubles of the Mexican Americans he served. César grew to trust Father McDonnell, and the priest had great respect for César. Father McDonnell introduced him to Mahatma Gandhi's ideas about nonviolent protest. César recognized how much in common those ideas had with the advice he had gotten from his mother so long ago, to use his mind instead of his fists.

The other important man César met in *Sal Si Puedes* was Fred Ross. Ross worked with the Community Service Organization (CSO). The CSO knew that there was power in the vote. The first important job Chávez had with the CSO was helping to register four thousand new voters.

These voters helped to elect a Mexican American representative to the city council so that the voice of their community might be heard. César realized what gaining a voice in the government could accomplish, and so he volunteered to work with the CSO. After working all day, César knocked on doors all night, encouraging his fellow Mexican American citizens to vote. In 1958 César became director of the CSO.

The people of *Sal Si Puedes* often lacked basic services, such as indoor plumbing.

## *Viva La Causa!*
## "Long live the cause!"

In 1962 César left his job at the CSO to pursue an even bigger dream. He had never forgotten the hard life that he lived as a migrant farm worker. He knew that the people who worked in the fields, gathering the harvests to feed the nation, had a right to be paid fairly for their hard labor and to be treated with dignity and respect. This would be his life's cause: to ensure a better life for the farm workers of America.

The Chávez family moved to Delano, California, where Helen had family and where César's brother Richard lived. Here he formed the National Farm Workers Association (NFWA). To support the family while the union was being set up, César and his wife returned to work in the fields, harvesting grapes.

In 1965 the NFWA took a stand in support of striking grape harvesters. César made sure the union members understood that all demonstrations were to be nonviolent. They would raise their voices and speak their minds to convince people of their cause.

The voices of the NFWA were heard loud and clear. Many people supported the cause by agreeing not to buy the grapes sold by companies that did not treat their workers fairly.

The arguments of the NFWA in support of better working conditions for farm laborers and their belief in nonviolent protest gained the attention of Senator Robert F. Kennedy, a Democrat from New York. Senator Kennedy supported the NFWA. He criticized the local sheriff for his treatment of the strikers, and he remained an important ally, or partner, of the NFWA.

**Senator Robert F. Kennedy and César Chávez (both seated), in early 1968. Kennedy would be assassinated later that year. César was deeply hurt by his death.**

On March 17, 1966, César and seventy other members of the NFWA began a march of over three hundred miles from Delano to Sacramento, the state capital of California. They marched for *La Causa,* the Cause.

As the marchers followed the NFWA banner, with its proud eagle, from town to town, more supporters joined the march. People all over the country watched the marchers on television. Americans were impressed with the dedication of the marchers, and they listened to what the NFWA had to say about the working conditions in the grape vineyards. The marchers asked that people not buy grapes from companies that treated their employees unfairly. They urged buyers to look for the NFWA eagle on the grapes they bought.

Finally, there was a breakthrough. Schenley Industries, one of the country's largest grape growers, agreed to sign a contract, or agreement, with the farm workers' union. This was the first contract for farm workers ever signed in the United States.

The Schenley contract did not bring an end to the struggle. Strikes, demonstrations, and **boycotts** against nonunion grape growers continued so that more farm workers could enjoy the protection of a contract.

César marched in 1966, and met with strikers in 1968, to encourage nonviolence.

By 1968 some strikers were turning to violence. César found guns on one picket line, and someone burned a number of packing sheds belonging to a grape grower. The people were forgetting César's lessons about the importance of nonviolence. Something, he decided, must be done to remind the members of the NFWA and their supporters that only peaceful acts would bring them nearer to a better life for everyone.

Following the example of Gandhi, César Chávez stopped eating. He called a meeting to explain that he would fast until union members recommitted themselves to nonviolence. The **fast** also showed he would not be promoting the grape industry, or consuming grapes, from which supermarkets profited. Once again, César had the attention of the country. Martin Luther King Jr. and Robert Kennedy both expressed their support. On the **predetermined** date of March 10, 1968, César stopped fasting.

## A Reason to Celebrate

It was clear that the strikes and the boycotts of nonunion growers were paying off. After Schenley signed the union contract, pressure on other growers continued. Finally, in July 1970, César could make an exciting announcement: Twenty-three companies were ready to negotiate with the union. By the mid-1970s, two-thirds of grape growers in California were under contract with César's union.

**César's brother Richard holds the first crate of Coachella Valley grapes to display the union logo.**

Thanks to César, his union, and its supporters, the workers in the grape vineyards got a hiring hall, which meant the end of discrimination by labor contractors. Higher wages, protection against pesticides, and other benefits were negotiated too. With great ceremony, the agreements were signed.

César and his followers had completed an important mission, but there were other struggles ahead. *La Causa* had never been just about the workers in the grape vineyards—it was about the plight of all poor people.

## The Legacy of César Chávez

César Chávez would continue his work for more than twenty years after the triumph of July 1970. In fact, before a month had passed, he was organizing the lettuce workers. Once again, a boycott was called. When a judge ordered César to call off the boycott, he refused, was fined, and spent twenty days in jail.

César was now a public figure of great importance, but many people did not agree with what he was doing for the workers. He received death threats and was convinced by others that he should have guard dogs to protect him. But no matter what the challenge—or even the threat—César Chávez never wavered from his belief in nonviolence. There would be more demonstrations, strikes, and fasts for what he believed in, but never would he raise his hand against another. He never forgot the advice of his mother, to use his mind instead of his fists.

# Saying Farewell to a Hero

Richard Chávez had run and swam and played with his brother César when they were young, before their family lost their small businesses and precious land. He worked beside him in the fields and on the picket lines. In the end, Richard built his brother's casket. It was a simple pine box that was carried during César's funeral, along with the union's banner bearing its proud black eagle, and the flags of Mexico and the United States.

Approximately forty thousand people would pay their last respects to this man on the day of his funeral. His mourners followed the banners and the handmade casket for more than three miles. They walked along part of the route that César had traveled for *La Causa*, a route that had led many to self-respect and better lives for themselves and their families.

**Statue of César Chávez at California State University**

# Now Try This

## A Banner for Identity

What might a banner that represented your school or your class look like? César Chávez and his farm workers' union followed a banner to declare their group identity when they demonstrated and marched. That banner was designed by César's brother, Richard, with the help of a graphic designer. They decided to show an eagle on the banner because an eagle appears on the Mexican flag. Some say that the eagle they designed has the look of an ancient Aztec temple, bringing to mind the ancient culture of Mexico. César chose the colors for the banner: Black stood for the struggles of the farm workers, red for the sacrifices that they would make, and white for hope.

The workers carried their banner proudly, telling everyone who they were and what they stood for.

## Here's How to Do It!

1. Think about images to represent the different backgrounds of people in your class and the different hobbies or special interests they might have.
2. Draw some pictures for your banner, or gather photographs or pictures from magazines.
3. What do you all have in common? Consider how you might represent this with a drawing or other image.
4. Choose two or three colors that have a special meaning to the group. What do your colors represent to you?
5. Decide what your group is called. You might also decide to use a slogan.
6. Create your banner!

# Glossary

**boycotts** *v.* refusals to buy or use a product or service.

**discrimination** *n.* act of showing an unfair difference in treatment.

**fast** *v.* to go without food; eat little or nothing.

**grueling** *adj.* very tiring; exhausting.

**predetermined** *v.* determined or decided beforehand.

**strikes** *n.* acts of stopping work.